CCSS Genre Fiction

MW00451821

Essential Question
How do people get along?

PARTNERS

by Jerome Anderson
illustrated by Penny Weber

CHAPTER 1 A Project

Mrs. Fuller stood in front of the class. "Boys and girls," she said, "I want to spend our science time today talking about the science fair. I know some of you were in it last year, but the rules are a bit different this year. This year, you may work with a partner, so pick someone who you think will be able to cooperate with you."

Ella turned around in her chair to look at her best friend, Lizzie. She was amused to see Lizzie already looking at her. "Partners?" she mouthed, and she grinned when Lizzie nodded quickly. She turned back around to listen to Mrs. Fuller explain how to do the projects.

Ella had won a second-place ribbon last year. This year, she wanted to win a blue ribbon *and* a purple Best in Show ribbon. She couldn't wait to get started with Lizzie. Lizzie was not always the most patient person, but she was really good at science.

After school, Ella and Lizzie climbed onto the bus together. Before Ella had a chance to say anything, Lizzie said, "I have the best project idea!"

"I have one, too!" Ella said. "We can show how flowers drink water."

"We can show how seeds move," Lizzie said at the same time.

The girls sat in silence for a moment. Lizzie said, "My brother did the project with seeds, and it was really cool. He put on socks and walked through the park to see which seeds stuck to him."

Ella smiled faintly. "My sister did the flower project with white carnations and put different colors of food coloring in their water. Then she used flower cutouts on her board."

"Oh," Lizzie said. "I guess we'll have to choose one or the other."

"Yeah," Ella said. "How are we going to pick which one is better?"

"Well, I did a project last year, and I won a blue ribbon. How did you do?" Lizzie said.

Ella looked down and mumbled, "I got a second-place ribbon."

"Then we should definitely use my idea," Lizzie announced. "This is my stop! See you tomorrow," she called as she got off the bus.

Ella thought about the project for the rest of the afternoon. She had really wanted to do the flower project. She remembered it had looked interesting when her sister did it.

But maybe Lizzie was right and the seed idea was better. And maybe Ella would get to plan and design their display board. She loved doing creative things like that, and she knew she had a great imagination.

On Saturday, Ella and Lizzie went to the park to collect seeds. They each put on two old pairs of thick socks and walked sock-footed across the grass. After several passes through the peaceful field, the girls sat down to examine their feet.

"Look at my feet!" Lizzie said. "It's like the socks threw a party and entertained all the seeds. The seeds had so much fun, they didn't want to leave!" She laughed. "See this burr? It's got a bunch of little hooks to grab my sock, and it won't let go!"

"Here's a different kind," Ella said, pulling a spiky seed off her sock. "It's got little pointy parts. Ouch!"

"I think we should pull off the seeds and stick them on a piece of paper," Lizzie said. "We can make a chart and describe each kind of seed."

"And we can tell what kind of animals pick up the seeds on their fur," Ella said. "I can draw pictures of the animals!"

"No, I don't think that's a good idea," said Lizzie. "Drawing pictures is for little kids. I think it will look better if we find pictures on the computer. Besides, it will be a piece of cake to find plenty of pictures."

"But I'm good at drawing animals," Ella protested. "Remember I drew that picture of your dog, and you said it looked just like him?"

"I know," Lizzie said, "but if we want to win Best in Show, everything has to be perfect. Come on, let's get the seeds off."

Ella frowned as she pulled seeds off her socks. She thought the judges in the science fair would like that she had worked hard on the drawings, but maybe Lizzie was right. Maybe pictures from the computer would look better.

CHAPTER  4 Together

The next weekend, Lizzie went to Ella's house to put together their project display. Ella was excited about this part. She and her mother had chosen the display board and big stick-on letters. She had colored paper to write on, and she knew just where on the board she wanted to put the information. She could hardly wait to get started.

Ella wanted to show Lizzie all the materials and explain her ideas, but as she began to talk, Lizzie cut her off. "No. I think we should do it like this," Lizzie said. She started moving pictures and letters. When she uncapped a marker and prepared to write on the board, Ella cried, "Stop! I can't stand it any more!"

"What's the matter?" Lizzie asked, surprised.

"You haven't listened to any of my ideas about this project," Ella said. "I wanted to do the flower project, but we did your idea instead. I wanted to draw pictures, but no, we had to find them on the computer instead. Now you don't even care about my ideas for the board. This is not a very good team project." Ella was trying very hard not to cry.

Lizzie was quiet. Then she took a deep breath and said, "I'm sorry, Ella. You are right. I've been so worried about winning that I have not been a very good partner. We should be working together, and that means we should each get to use our ideas. You are much better than I am at doing art projects, so we should definitely use your ideas for the board."

Ella smiled at her friend. "Thank you! I think you will like my ideas."

The girls worked happily together for the rest of the afternoon. Their display board looked wonderful, and as they finished up, Lizzie looked excitedly at Ella. "Even if we don't end up winning, we still make a pretty good team!" she said. "But I think we *will* win Best in Show!"

"I hope so, partner!" Ella replied with a grin.

And they did.

Summarize

Use important details to help you summarize *Partners*.

Character	Clue	Point of View

Text Evidence

1. How do you know *Partners* is fiction? GENRE

2. What does Ella think about working with Lizzie in the first part of the story? How do you know? POINT OF VIEW

3. Use context clues to figure out the meaning of the idiom "a piece of cake" on page 9. IDIOMS

4. Write about how Lizzie and Ella learn to work together. Give details. WRITE ABOUT READING

Compare Texts

Read about an organization that helps kids learn and work together.

The first 4-H clubs focused on country life.

In the early 1900s, a group of clubs for boys and girls started. These clubs used the idea of "hands-on" learning. They taught new ideas about farming to young people who lived in rural areas.

J. Baylor Roberts/Alamy

4-H members make friends, learn life skills, and help their communities.

Today, 4-H clubs have millions of members all across the United States. Boys and girls from elementary school through high school still learn by doing. The clubs focus on leadership, science, and healthy living. Members interact with each other and their communities.

THE 4 H'S STAND FOR HEAD, HEART, HANDS, AND HEALTH.

Courtesy of 4-H National Headquarters at the National Institute of Food and Agriculture (NIFA)

Clubs plan and do their own projects. Some clubs focus on animal science. They raise and show animals. Others focus on activities like using computers, gardening, cooking, or making crafts.

You name it, and a 4-H club can do it!

Some 4-H programs in animal science teach skills to kids who want to be veterinarians.

Make Connections

Why is it important to cooperate with a partner?
ESSENTIAL QUESTION

How do both stories show people getting along and cooperating? TEXT TO TEXT

Focus on Social Studies

Purpose To find out why it is important for people to cooperate

What to Do

Step 1 Find out about a group in your community that helps people cooperate. It might be a group you are already part of, such as a team or a scout troop. Or, you might choose another group to find out about.

Step 2 Write a paragraph telling about the group. Tell what it does and how it helps people get along together. Be sure to include details that show why this group is interesting.